Reflections of the North

Reflections of the North

Stoddart

Published in Canada in 1991 by
Stoddart Publishing Co. Limited
34 Lesmill Road
Toronto, Canada
M3B 2T6

Published by arrangement with
NorthWord Press, Inc.

Canadian Cataloguing in Publication Data

Main entry under title:

Reflections of the north

ISBN 0-7737-2541-5

1. Canada, Northern - Description and travel - Views.
2. Natural history - Canada, Northern - Pictorial works. I. Klein, Tom, 1947-

FC3956.R44 1991   917.19'0022'2   C91-094588-8
F1090.5.R44 1991

Designed by Mary Shafer
Photograph editing by Bob Baldwin
Text editing by Tom Klein

Printed and bound in Hong Kong by Book Art

Reflections of the North
is dedicated to all
who have worked tirelessly to protect
the wilderness character of the northland

ACKNOWLEDGEMENTS

The editors thank the many contributors to *Reflections of the North*.
The photographs were selected from submissions of many hundreds of
images by the north country's finest outdoor and wildlife photo-
graphers. The visual power of the book rests upon the patience and
perseverance of these artists.

The text comes courtesy of a broad range of writers and thinkers
over a broad range of time. Whether 17th-century fur traders or
contemporary writers, these people have thought deeply about the
nature of the north. Their reflections provide a framework for this
northern adventure.

NORTHWORDS

AN INTRODUCTION

In Portage, Wisconsin, there is a prominent sign in a roadside park. It states plainly and proudly: "Where the North Begins." Portage rests well south of the 44th Parallel. It's a mere thirty-five miles north of Madison, the state capitol, and about 180 miles north of Chicago — hardly the hub of the north.

But maybe there's some truth here. The Portage sign, a chamber of commerce slogan, went up in the 1930s. In the '30s, even in Southern Wisconsin, you could find solitude, wildlife and undisturbed ecosystems. Back then, along the Wisconsin River bottoms near Portage, all these elements were present. Today an enormous power plant smoke-stack is visible from the "Where the North Begins" sign. The river on a hot summer day is alive with people. Let's be kind and concede that Portage might be "Where the North *Once Began.*"

So where is north now? While north is a state of mind rather than a line on the map, "northness" does evoke predictable images. Ask anyone who loves the north. They will speak of smoky gold tamaracks on sunny October days, bold granite outcrops erupting from pristine blue lakes, a moose swimming across a quiet bay at sunset, or of a stand of white pines old enough to remember the *chansons* of the voyageurs. They may also describe, or try to describe, the visual symphony of northern lights at twenty below, the impossibly white head and tail of a soaring eagle, a lake trout dancing on a light rod, and of course, the echoing call of a loon breaking the stillness of a northern night. These are the images of "The North." You might encounter some of these sights and sounds in northern Illinois, central Pennsylvania or even in the Pine Barrens of New Jersey.

To find the whole package, though, you have to travel beyond the cities, suburbs and farms. I've always believed that the north begins where the cornfields stop. Perhaps we can best define it by what is missing. Like golden arches, shopping malls, car washes, movie theaters, four-lane highways and easy money. Those who live in the north don't worry much about those missing amenities. There are plenty of Big Macs in Milwaukee, Boston, Detroit, New York, Chicago and other concrete canyons to the south. Anyway, those "EAT" signs on the roofs of backwoods bars have character. And if you want your car washed, you can always wait for rain.

In the pages of *Reflections of the North* you will encounter the northern experience. You will absorb the sounds, the silence, the pristine landscapes, the pure waters. You will probably recall your own northern adventures, and experience that inexorable magnetic pull to the north. Follow the compass of your soul. It doesn't matter if your north is New Hampshire's lake country, the Minnesota/Ontario border country, Alaska's back country or the bush country of the Northwest Territories. What counts is how this country *feels*. You have to want and need the simple feeling of being there. As Mark Peterson, Director of the Sigurd Olson Environmental Institute, describes so insightfully (p.52), we may argue about where the north precisely begins, but "we instinctively know when we've arrived." Mark learned about the north from the master, wilderness crusader and author Sigurd F. Olson. Olson was the most profound and poetic of all northern writers, capturing the north in many timeless metaphors. His evocative descriptions of the "singing wilderness" define the essence of the northwoods. For Sig Olson and many others, the north is a spiritual home. It has quiet power. It works slowly and relentlessly on your psyche. It gets into your blood, your *soul*.

While the north is powerful, it is also fragile. Its wild country is a delicate community. We must fight the urge to absorb too much of it, to hold it so tightly that we squeeze the life out of it. We must keep development forces in check. One more lakeshore chopped into two-acre "estates"; one more innocent gravel road bulldozed into the woods; another fly-in camp planted in a pristine wilderness may be small changes individually, but collectively they change the face of the north. The north does "keep getting farther north every year."

Just look at the loon's story. For many the symbol of the north, the common loon has lost a lot of ground. At the turn of this century, loons nested south to the 42nd Parallel – a line running roughly from the northern California border to northern Illinois to northern Connecticut. At the turn of the next century, loons will be lucky to hold the 45th Parallel in most of their range – a loss of nearly 300 miles. Did we really lose that much of the north over the past century? Can we hold the line in the 21st century? These are questions not for scientists who study range maps, but for us – people who cherish the spirit of the north. Let's draw the line now.

– Tom Klein, 1991
Minocqua, Wisconsin

My father, you have spoken well; you have told me that heaven is very beautiful; tell me now one thing more. Is it more beautiful than the country of the musk ox in summer, when sometimes the mist blows over the lakes, and sometimes the water is blue, and the loons cry very often? -

— Saltatha, a Yellowknife Indian

cosystems are like intimate human relationships; the components need and nourish each other while demanding independence and space; changes in one bring about changes in the other, there are phases and cycles, the changes tuned to time; and there are constants represented by the life processes that make it possible for the systems to flourish in different forms when trauma disrupts or removes a component. Just as human relationships mature over years, so do ecosystem communities over a longer period. A big tree forest, for example, comes into being over several centuries.

— Robert Trever

here Leopold once saw the fierce green fire in the dying wolf's eyes we can look into the eyes of the black bear more closely and see it - alive. What we see is almost incomprehensible. But not quite. We are, after all, just beginning to learn about our world again, the second time around. Poised between a past we cannot afford to lose and a mountain of impending truth, we find ourselves in another type of Kawishiwi country - this no place between - by a rapid river flowing across the broad and factual continent of our intelligence. Searching for our bearings. Circling overhead, in a stellar performance mocking our own lives, the great skybear stalks her infinite territory, followed forever by a single cub who carries true North in the tip of his tail.

— Jeff Fair

Only to the white man was nature a wilderness and only to him was the land 'infested' with 'wild' animals and 'savage' people. To us it was tame. Earth was bountiful and we were surrounded with the blessings of the Great Mystery.

– Chief Luther Standing Bear
of the Oglala Sioux

 am glad I shall never be young without wild country to be young in. What avail are forty freedoms without a blank spot on the map?

— Aldo Leopold

The North keeps getting further north every year.

— Anonymous

nce in his life a man ought to concentrate his mind upon the remembered earth. He ought to give himself up to a particular landscape in his experience; to look at it from as many angles as he can, to wonder upon it, to dwell upon it. He ought to imagine that he touches it with his hands at every season and listens to the sounds that are made upon it. He ought to imagine the creatures there and all the faintest motions of the wind. He ought to recollect the glare of the moon and the colors of the dawn and dusk.

– N. Scott Momaday

For the animal shall not be measured by man. In a world older and more complete than ours they move finished and complete, gifted with extensions of the senses we have lost or never attained, living by voices we shall never hear. They are not brethren, they are not underlings; they are other nations, caught with ourselves in the net of life and time, fellow prisoners of the splendor and travail of the earth.

– Henry Beston

*I*s not the sky a father
and the earth a mother
and are not all living things
with feet or wings or roots their
children?

— Black Elk

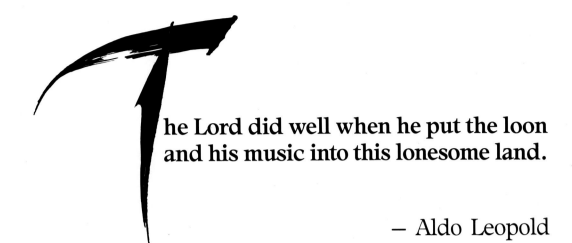

The Lord did well when he put the loon
and his music into this lonesome land.

— Aldo Leopold

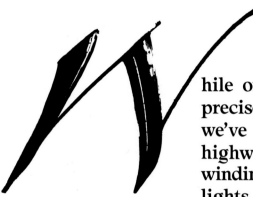hile one can argue about where the north precisely begins, we instinctively know when we've arrived. In the North the ribbons of highways to the south are replaced by winding rivers. Instead of the neon and amber lights of downstate cities are stars in the heavens above so bright that they seem nearer to the earth. The howl of the wolf or call of the coyote is more likely to be heard than the siren of a police car or the thunder of a jet. A defining difference, quite simply, is that in the northwoods there are more white-tailed deer than Fords, more lakes than shopping malls.

– Mark Peterson

We once knew the wolf. We behaved as it did. We tried to capture some of its spirit, to learn from it how to hunt, and the social rules of the hunting group. We must have learned well, for we are still here, thriving, after a fashion, and we have no more need for the teacher.

— Denny Olson

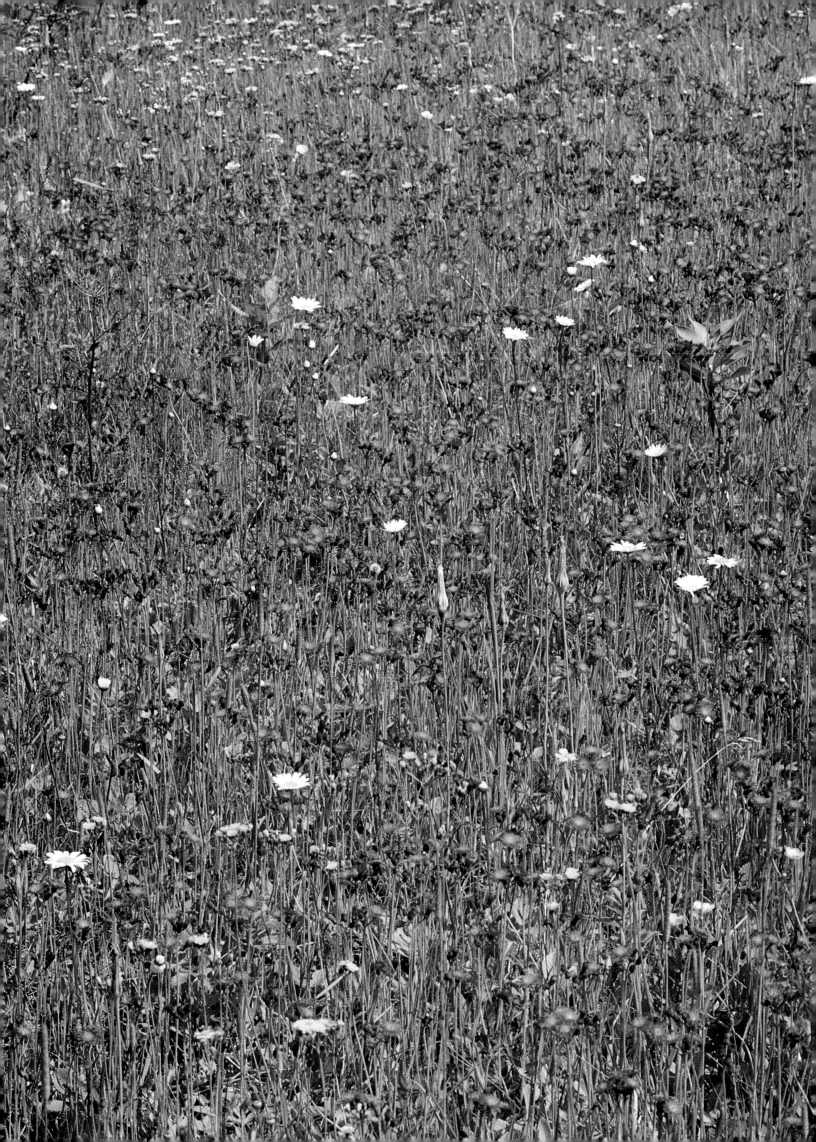

The northwoods is one of the most recently uncovered places in the world. Less than 10,000 years ago, while civilization was well underway in the Middle East, parts of the northwoods were still under an ice cap that stood two miles high in places. The enormous weight of the ice caused the lower layer to bulge outward in all directions, bulldozing mountains and gouging the earth as it moved. Frigid air swooped down from the front of the glacier, creating a wide fringe of tundra wherever it went. When the glacier finally stopped and began to melt backwards, great muddy torrents roared over its cliffs and rushed out through tunnels in its face. Their payload of crushed rock, gravel, sand and ice settled over hundreds of miles to form the lake-splattered landscape that we know today.

— Janine Benyus

I have always been impressed by the scale and grandeur of the canoe country. It is a hard and boney land and, were it not for the linking waterways of the area, would scarcely be penetrable. Unlike the grand vistas of mountain country, the canoe country allows you only glimpses of its magnitude. Almost furtively it leads you on, down narrow lakes or winding rivers, opening itself only gradually to the explorer. One can sit atop a mountain and contemplate an entire region; in the canoe country one sits only on small lichen-covered knobs, surveying intimate scenes. But it is exactly this shyness that is the canoe country's charm and one must probe it slowly and over long years before knowing many of its secrets, before sensing its grandeur.

– Michael Furtman

In our everyday world of human-made, human-scale things, we are inclined to think rather well of ourselves. We are *Homo sapiens*, after all, and even in this day of evolutionary enlightenment generally view ourselves as favored offspring of the universe. It takes an eagle to bring us down to size. Though only a fraction of our weight, these birds dwarf us; for by soaring into the sky, they give a tangible, vertical dimension to the observable world. They offer us a measure of the heavens and, as they disappear above the clouds, hint at spheres beyond our sphere to which we have no ready access. Perhaps we are not the center of things after all, not so very large, not so powerful. With all the finesse of modern technology, we can't ride the air like the eagles. We can't even come close.

— Candace Savage

I have seen maybe a thousand northern lakes, and they all look alike in many ways, but there was something different about that little lake that held me hard. I sat there perhaps half an hour, like a man under a spell, just looking it over.

– John J. Rowlands

The singing wilderness has to do with the calling of the loons, northern lights, and the great silences of a land lying north of Lake Superior. It is concerned with the simple joys, the timelessness and the perspective found in a way of life that is close to the past. I have discovered that I am not alone in my listening; that almost everyone is listening for something, that the search for places where the singing may be heard goes on everywhere. It seems to be part of the hunger that all of us have for a time when we were closer to lakes and rivers, to mountains and meadows and forests, than we are today. . .We may not know exactly what it is we are listening for, but we hunt as instinctively for opportunities and places to listen as sick animals look for healing herbs.

— Sigurd F. Olson

lake is the landscape's most beautiful and expresssive feature. It is earth's eye; looking into which the beholder measures the depth of his own nature. The fluviatile trees next the shore are the slender eyelashes which fringe it, and the wooded hills and cliffs around are its overhanging brows.

— Henry David Thoreau

It's very sad if our culture only sees wilderness as a place to play. What wilderness should be doing is speaking to our souls and teaching us about being quiet...and respecting the world we live in.

— Bill Mason

ur tent is on the northern tip of the island. We look out past a great sweep of pine bough to the waters of our lake and the silent misty one beyond. This is the moment, I think, when I've really given my heart to our canoe country, though I've been entranced with it from the first. But here its special quality of wild innocence touches me sharply and deeply.

– Florence Page Jacques

ears ago, a friend who lived on the seashore was shocked to learn that the admired scent of salt air was due in part to the odor of decomposing marine organisms. But knowing this should not detract from anyone's fun at the beach, where, after all, the sun still shines as brightly, and the waves still break into foam. Nor should it detract from our enjoyment of the woods to know that brilliant fall colors foretell the imminent wholesale death of once-green leaves preparing to go to earth and decay. It might even heighten our enjoyment of autumn, by lending a sense of urgency to the task of getting out into the country before the colors fade and the trees drop their foliage. In recent years more people than ever have apparently felt this urgency, because autumn foliage has been attracting tourists and travelers by the millions to wooded areas. Each fall the inns are filled, buses are chartered, cars crowd the highways, and bikers and hikers hit the roads and trails as legions of leaf-peepers open their eyes to nature's extravagance. And extravagance it seems to be, for there appears to be no good reason for a tree to take on scarlet, gold or wine. A brilliant flower can attract the pollinating insect or bird it needs for the plant's reproduction, but a brilliant leaf attracts only the gaze of its admirer.

— Ron Lanner

The North Country is a siren. Who can resist her song of intricate and rich counterpoint - the soaring harmonies of bird melodies against an accompaniment of lapping waters, roaring cataracts, and the soft, sad overtones of pine boughs? Her flowing garments are forever green, the rich velvet verdure of pine needles. In autumn she pricks out the green background with embroidery of gold here and scarlet there. Winter adds a regal touch, with gleaming diamonds in her hair and ermine billowing from her shoulders. Those who have ever seen her in her beauty or listened to her vibrant melodies can never quite forget her nor lose the urge to return to her.

— Grace Lee Nute

It is snowing today. The scent of the snow is manifest. The spruce are powdered deep, that soft plumes of the great white pines are overlaid with films of silver. White flakes tumble thick and fast, brushing against my face like evanescent butterflies. All the peace that this country has given us comes showering down around us in the heavy snowfall. Our departure, in this mood, is beautiful to me. Without a pang I see the myriad footprints, which we have made along our shore and in the ice-held forest, vanish beneath the drifting snowflakes.

– Florence Page Jaques

Many people clearly recall their first experience with loons, and people almost always remember the first time they heard loon music. I'm slightly embarrassed to admit I don't. While boyhood trips to northern Wisconsin produced a few loon encounters, nothing special happened. It wasn't until August of 1965 on the Minnesota-Canada border that loons grabbed my soul. With Bill Richtsmeier, a high school buddy, I drove to Moose Lake, a little ways north of Ely, to start a great Boundary Waters adventure. After a long day's paddle and portage, we made it to Louisa Falls at the bottom of Agnes Lake, just over the Canadian border. Shoulders bright red from the August sun and sore from the sharp bite of the thin Duluth pack straps, we settled into the campsite surrounded by a reassuring audio backdrop of falling water. The loons on Agnes called that night, probably no louder nor more often than they do on any other August night. But the calling found the right spot. We sat by the campfire bewitched, anticipating two weeks of granite cliffs, water diamonds on the shimmering lakes, firm lake trout, spongy sphagnum moss and quiet evenings with the voices of the wilderness. That night on Agnes we didn't know the difference between the tremolo, wail or yodel. And we didn't care. We just soaked it all in. It was a magical night. I haven't kept track of Bill over the passing years so I can't speak for him, but nothing has been the same for me since.

— Tom Klein

n this winter night, the wilderness waits - a reservoir of silence and darkness held for safekeeping in a world of noise and streetlights. It is a gift to the few who live along its edge, and to many who do not. Perhaps most importantly, it is a gift held in trust for those whose lives have not yet begun. The wolves are its night watchmen, the stars its only lamps.

– David Olesen

The way of the canoe is the way of the wilderness and of a freedom almost forgotten. It is an antidote to insecurity, the open door to waterways of ages past and a way of life with profound and abiding satisfactions. When a man is part of his canoe, he is part of all that canoes have ever known.

— Sigurd F. Olson

I rejoice that there are owls. Let them do the idiotic and maniacal hooting for men. It is a sound admirably suited to swamps and twilight woods which no day illustrates, suggesting a vast and undeveloped nature which men have not recognized. They represent the stark twilight and unsatisfied thoughts which we all have.

– Henry David Thoreau

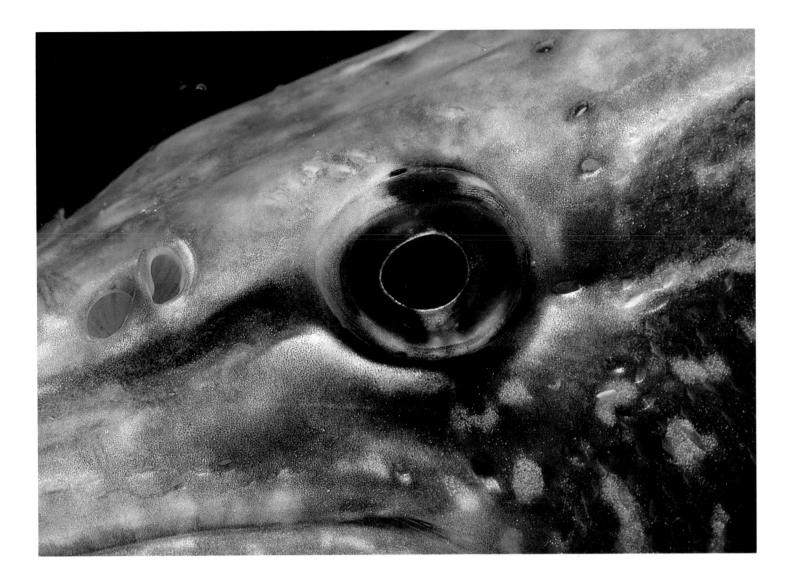

It is something to be alone in the bush, the wind in the trees and the feeling that if there are such things as big cities, they must have existed in some ancient past. It is a fine thing to climb a rise, sit in the weeds, smoke a pipe and look off for miles at more of the same country you just came through.

– Gordon MacQuarrie

omething lost behind the ranges,
Something hidden, go and find it.
Go and look behind the ranges,
Something lost behind the ranges,
Lost and waiting for you. Go.

– Rudyard Kipling

And the evening sun descending
Set the clouds on fire with redness,
Burned the broad sky like a prairie
Left upon the level water
One long track and trail of splendor
Down whose stream, as down a river,
Westward, westward Hiawatha
Sailed into the fiery sunset
Sailed into the purple vapors
Sailed into the dusk of evening.

– Longfellow

ut can't you hear the wild?
    It's calling you.
    Let us probe the silent places,
    Let us seek the luck betide us;
Let us journey to a lonely land I know.
There's a whisper on the night wind,
There's a star agleam to guide us,
And the Wind is calling. . .
Let us go.

— Robert Service

orth is a state of mind, not a geographic delineation.

-Tom Klein

bove all, it is wild nature itself in this region that charms. To be able to follow unfamiliar water-courses days, weeks and months, to contend with wind and wave, to sleep in the open under pines or beside leaping water, to view sun and shadow on the changing scene of woodland, rock, and water, to hobnob with the wild creatures of the north, in short to lose oneself in the profusion of original America - all this is the cherished dream of every true American.

— Ernest C. Oberholtzer

This is a delicious evening, when the whole body is one sense, and imbibes delight through every pore. I go and come with a strange liberty in Nature, a part of herself. As I walk along the stony shore of the pond in my shirt sleeves, though it is cool as well as cloudy and windy, and I see nothing special to attract me, all the elements are unusually congenial to me. The bull frogs trump to usher in the night, and the note of the whippoorwill is borne on the rippling wind from over the water. Sympathy with the fluttering alder and poplar leaves almost takes away my breath; yet, like the lake, my serenity is rippled but not ruffled.

— Henry David Thoreau

There's gold, and it's haunting
and haunting;
It's luring me on as of old;
Yet it isn't the gold that I'm wanting
So much as just finding the gold.
It's the great, big, broad land
'way up yonder,
It's the forests where silence has lease;
It's the beauty that thrills me with wonder,
It's the stillness that fills me with peace.

– Robert Service

To anyone has spent a winter in the north and known the depths to which the snow can reach, known the weeks when the mercury stays below zero, the first hint of spring is a major event. You must live in the north to understand it. You cannot just come up for it as you might go to Florida for the sunshine and the surf. To appreciate it, you must go through considerable enduring.

— Sigurd F. Olson

No one can weigh or measure culture, hence I shall waste no time trying to do so. Suffice it to say that by common consent of thinking people, there are cultural values in the sports, customs and experiences that renew contacts with wild things.

– Aldo Leopold

Appears to have been much frequented by the savages of old, as may be judged from the various figures of animals & c. made by them on the face of the steep Rock. Amongst them may be seen fish, flesh, and Tortoise all of them painted with some kind of Red Paint. These figures are made by scratching the Rock weed (moss) off the Rocks with the Point of a knife or some other instrument.

— John Macdonell

ur ability to perceive quality in nature begins, as in art, with the pretty. It expands through successive stages of the beautiful to values as yet uncaptured by language.

— Aldo Leopold

We need to preserve a few places, a few samples of primeval country so that when the pace gets too fast we can look at it, think about it, contemplate it, and somehow restore equanimity to our souls.

– Sigurd F. Olson

TEXT SOURCES

Intro.   Tom Klein

Page 12   Quoted in Warburton Pike, *The Barren Ground of Northern Canada*, London, 1892

Page 17   From *Voyageur Country*, University of Minnesota Press, 1979

Page 21   From *The Great American Bear*, NorthWord Press, Inc., 1990

Page 25   Quoted from *The Great American Bear*, NorthWord Press, Inc., 1990

Page 28   From *Round River*, Oxford University Press, 1953

Page 32   Anonymous, but well said

Page 37   Quoted from *Arctic Dreams*, Charles Scribner's Sons, 1986

Page 40   Quoted from *Caribou and The Barren Lands*, Canadian Arctic Resources Committee, 1981

Page 45   From *Black Elk Speaks*, University of Nebraska Press, 1932

Page 49   From *Round River*, Oxford University Press, 1953

Page 52   From an article in the *Wisconsin Academy Review*, 1989

Page 56   From *Wolves*, NorthWord Press, Inc., 1990

Page 61   From the *Northwoods Wildlife Guide*, NorthWord Press, Inc., 1989

Page 64   From *A Season for Wilderness*, NorthWord Press, Inc., 1989

Page 68   From *Eagles of North America*, NorthWord Press, Inc., 1987

Page 73   From *Cache Lake Country*, W.W. Norton and Company, 1947

Page 76   From *The Singing Wilderness*, Alfred A. Knopf, 1956

Page 80   From *Walden*, 1854

Page 85   *Path of the Paddle*, Key Porter Books, 1984

Page 88   From *Canoe Country*, University of Minnesota Press, 1938

Page 93   From *Autumn Leaves*, NorthWord Press, Inc., 1990

Page 96   From *The Voyager's Highway*, The Minnesota Historical Society, 1941

Page 101   From *Snowshoe Country*, The University of Minnesota Press, 1944

Page 105   From *Loon Magic*, NorthWord Press, Inc., 1985

Page 109   From an article in the *Boundary Waters Canoe Area Wilderness News*, 1981

Page 112   From *The Singing Wilderness*, Alfred A. Knopf, 1956

Page 117   From *Walden*, 1854

Page 120   From *Stories of the Old Duck Hunter*, Willow Creek Press, 1985

Page 124   From *The Explorer*, 1894

Page 129   From the *Song of Hiawatha*, 1855

Page 132   From the *Call of the Wild*, 1907

Page 136   From *Living in the North, Wisconsin Natural Resources*, 1982

Page 141   From an address to the North American Game Conference, 1929.

Page 146   From the *Spell of the Yukon*, 1907

Page 149   From *The Singing Wilderness*, Alfred A. Knopf, 1956

Page 153   From *A Sand County Almanac*, Oxford University Press, 1949

Page 154   From the diary of fur trader, John Macdonell, 1793

Page 157   From *A Sand County Almanac*, Oxford University Press, 1949

Page 158   From an address to the Utah Academy of Sciences, 1958

PHOTOGRAPHER CREDITS

Photographer	Page
Robert Baldwin	10-11,13, 24, 31, 41, 48, 57, 60, 65, 77,108, 111, 115, 133, 138, 143, 144, Back Cover,89,67
Craig Blacklock	22, 66, 78-79, 113, 142
Don Blegen	114
Daniel J. Cox	20, 27, 51, 53, 97, 123, 127, 134-135
Michael Francis	36, 47
Michael Furtman	33, 155
John Gerlach	29, 38, 39, 42, 50, 86, 90, 100, 106, 130-131, 159
Gary Griffen	26, 35, 74, 84, 98, 121, 140, 147, Front Cover
Bill Kenney	43, 63, 83, 152
Steven J. Krasemann	46, 55, 69

Photographer	Page
Tim Leary	14
Karen Lollo	104
Bill Marchel	18, 34, 148, 150-151
Peggy Morsch	125
Scott Nielsen	2-3
Rod Planck	8, 15, 16, 23, 30, 58-59, 70, 82, 87, 92, 94-95, 99, 107, 110, 116, 118, 122, 126, 128, 156
Gregory Scott	71, 91
Ron Spomer	19, 139
Doug Stamm	119, 137
Lynn M. Stone	54, 81, 102-103, 160
Mark Wallner	62, 72, 75
Henry Zeman	44